E. A. COLLINS

Galactic Odyssey

First edition

This book was professionally typeset on Reedsy.
Find out more at reedsy.com

Contents

1

Mysterious Transmission

The dimly lit control room of the starship "Galactic Odyssey" hummed with anticipation as Captain Alex and the crew prepared for their next jump through the hyperspace gateway. The vast expanse of the cosmos stretched before them, an uncharted tapestry of stars and galaxies awaiting their exploration.

As the crew went about their tasks, Lieutenant Ramirez, the ship's communications expert, noticed an unusual signal flickering on the monitor. His eyes widened in surprise, and he called out to the captain, "Captain Alex, I think you should see this!"

Stepping over to Ramirez's station, Captain Alex furrowed his brow at the erratic transmission. The message was unlike anything they had encountered before—a pulsating sequence of encrypted data intertwined with alien symbols.

"What is it, Ramirez? Have you seen anything like this before?" the captain asked, his curiosity piqued.

The lieutenant shook his head, "No, sir. This transmission appears to be deliberately scrambled, and the source is unidentified. It's like nothing we've ever encountered."

The rest of the crew gathered around the communication console, intrigued by the mysterious signal. Commander Lee, the ship's second-in-command, suggested, "Should we attempt to decode it, Captain? It could be a distress signal or perhaps even a message from an advanced civilization."

Captain Alex weighed the options, knowing the transmission might contain invaluable information. "Proceed with caution, Commander. We mustn't underestimate the potential dangers of this signal. Begin decoding, but prioritize the safety of the ship and its crew."

As Lieutenant Ramirez began the decryption process, a sense of excitement and unease settled over the "Galactic Odyssey." Each passing moment heightened the suspense as they delved deeper into the enigma before them.

Hours turned into what felt like an eternity as the crew meticulously worked to unravel the transmission's secrets. With each layer of encryption peeled away, a new layer of complexity emerged, revealing glimpses of an unknown intelligence.

As the clock ticked on, the tension aboard the starship grew palpable. The crew members exchanged glances, their minds racing with questions and anticipation. What secrets did this enigmatic transmission hold? Were they on the brink of a momentous discovery, or were they unwittingly walking into a trap?

Captain Alex paced the control room, unable to shake the feeling that they were on the verge of something extraordinary. He knew that whatever lay concealed within that transmission could change the course of their entire expedition. However, he also understood the weight of responsibility that came with such knowledge—it could alter the delicate balance of power in the galaxy and draw unwanted attention to their mission.

With beads of sweat forming on his forehead, Lieutenant Ramirez finally cracked the final layer of encryption. The transmission's message materialized on the screen, a string of words in a language the crew had never seen before. The tension reached its peak as they stared at the message, unsure of its implications.

"Translate it, Ramirez," Captain Alex urged, his heart pounding in his chest.

The lieutenant's fingers flew across the console, utilizing every resource at their disposal to decipher the message. Finally, the words appeared in the universal language of the crew—English.

"Seek the Celestial Key. The fate of the galaxy depends on your journey. Trust no one, for darkness lurks in the cosmos. The enigma awaits."

Silence filled the control room as the weight of those words settled upon the crew. The journey of the "Galactic Odyssey" had just taken an unforeseen turn, and the path ahead was shrouded in mystery. With the transmission decoded, a new chapter in their odyssey began—one filled with suspense, danger, and the quest for the enigmatic Celestial Key.

2

The Hidden Agenda

The revelation of the mysterious transmission left the crew of the "Galactic Odyssey" both intrigued and apprehensive. The enigmatic message spoke of a Celestial Key and hinted at a hidden danger lurking in the cosmos. Captain Alex knew they couldn't take this information lightly, and suspicion grew among the crew.

As the starship continued its voyage through the vastness of space, unease settled among the crew members. Each person eyed their fellow shipmates with cautious curiosity, wondering who among them might be hiding a secret agenda. The cryptic message had left them all feeling exposed, unsure if any of them could be trusted.

Amidst the crew, a few individuals stood out, raising eyebrows and casting doubt on their intentions. Commander Lee, known for his exceptional skills in diplomacy and negotiation, seemed unusually reserved, avoiding eye contact and staying aloof from the others. Science Officer Dr. Evelyn Alvarez, who had a reputation for her remarkable intellect, had been spending long hours in the ship's research lab, leaving some crew members to wonder about the nature of her investigations.

Captain Alex found himself grappling with conflicting emotions. He had formed strong bonds with his crew, but the revelation of the transmission created an atmosphere of uncertainty and suspicion. He knew that to protect the mission and the crew's safety, he had to address the situation directly.

Gathering the core members of the crew in the ship's conference room, Captain Alex began, "We are on an unprecedented journey, one that may lead us to something of immense importance to the galaxy. The transmission we received spoke of a Celestial Key, and with it, great responsibility lies upon our shoulders. However, we must also face the reality that one among us might have their own agenda."

The room fell silent, the weight of the captain's words hanging in the air. Each person present considered the possibility that a traitor lurked within their midst. Trust had been the foundation of their success, and now it was under siege.

"We cannot allow paranoia to divide us," the captain continued. "Our mission demands unity and cooperation. But we must also be vigilant. I want each of you to report any unusual activities or suspicions immediately. We are a team, and we will face this challenge together."

The crew members nodded in agreement, acknowledging the gravity of the situation. They understood that their survival and the success of their mission depended on their ability to work together, to rise above the fear and uncertainty that threatened to consume them.

As days turned into weeks, the crew of the "Galactic Odyssey" grew more adept at maintaining a balance between their mission objectives and their personal apprehensions. Captain Alex encouraged team-building exercises and open communication to foster trust and camaraderie. Slowly, the crew began to feel a renewed sense of unity and determination.

Commander Lee and Dr. Alvarez, in particular, realized the importance of transparency. They opened up about their recent behavior, revealing that they had stumbled upon fragments of historical records during their research that hinted at the Celestial Key's existence. They had kept their findings to themselves, fearing they might be misinterpreted or trigger premature action.

Captain Alex appreciated their honesty, knowing that secrecy could have dire consequences. Together, they decided to share their discoveries with the entire crew, ensuring that everyone was on the same page and committed to facing whatever lay ahead as a united front.

As the "Galactic Odyssey" continued its voyage, the crew embraced their newfound trust, resolving to confront the mysteries of the Celestial Key together. The journey ahead was still shrouded in suspense, but the bond between the crew members had grown stronger, fortifying them against the darkness that lurked in the cosmos. With their resolve renewed, they set their sights on the next phase of their odyssey, determined to unlock the secrets that could shape the fate of the entire galaxy.

3

The Forbidden Planet

The "Galactic Odyssey" ventured deeper into the uncharted regions of space, following the clues left by the enigmatic transmission. Their voyage led them to a system teeming with celestial wonders, but it was a single planet that would capture their imagination and stir their sense of trepidation.

Lieutenant Alvarez, the ship's astrophysicist, had detected unusual energy readings emanating from a remote and seemingly uninhabited planet. As the crew conducted their preliminary scans, they discovered ancient ruins scattered across the planet's surface.

"Captain, you won't believe what we've found," Lieutenant Alvarez reported, her voice tinged with awe and excitement. "These ruins bear striking similarities to those of civilizations that existed millions of years ago. It's as if this planet was once a hub of advanced knowledge and technology."

Captain Alex's curiosity was piqued. "Is there any indication of who or what might have inhabited this place? Any signs of recent activity?"

Lieutenant Alvarez shook her head. "No signs of recent activity, Captain. It's like time itself swallowed this once-thriving civilization. The artifacts appear to be untouched for eons."

As the crew continued their exploration, they stumbled upon mysterious artifacts and intricate hieroglyphics, hinting at a long-lost culture that had surpassed the boundaries of known science. But among the ruins, they discovered something unsettling—a peculiar black obelisk, eerily pulsating with an otherworldly energy.

Science Officer Dr. Evelyn Alvarez cautioned, "Captain, this obelisk seems to be the source of the strange energy readings we detected earlier. It emits a powerful aura, almost like a gravitational field, but we can't decipher its purpose."

Despite the sense of wonder that permeated the team, there was an undeniable sense of unease. The planet's secrets felt ominous, as if ancient forces were watching their every move. Some crew members whispered of a malevolent presence, warning against meddling with forces beyond their comprehension.

As nightfall approached, the crew decided to set up camp near the ruins, hoping to continue their investigations at first light. However, the veil of darkness cast an eerie glow on the obelisk, and the crew began experiencing vivid and unsettling dreams, each person haunted by their deepest fears and regrets.

Commander Lee, usually stoic and composed, woke up in cold sweat, tormented by memories of a past negotiation gone awry. Lieutenant Ramirez found himself reliving the loss of a close friend during a space mission. Dr. Evelyn Alvarez saw haunting visions of her unresolved childhood trauma.

The crew realized that the obelisk was somehow influencing their minds, preying on their vulnerabilities and darkest memories. Captain Alex knew that they had to leave the planet immediately, but they couldn't afford to abandon the investigation either.

"We can't let this obelisk control us," Captain Alex declared, his voice resolute. "We must find a way to counter its influence and understand its purpose."

As they struggled to maintain their composure, they discovered an ancient text hidden among the ruins, describing the obelisk as a "Gateway to the Forbidden Cosmos." It warned of the immense power it held, capable of unraveling the very fabric of reality.

With the truth laid bare, the crew faced a choice—abandon the investigation and flee or confront the enigma that lay before them. The temptation of unraveling the mysteries of the Forbidden Cosmos was intoxicating, but the risks were equally grave.

Undeterred by the foreboding warnings, the "Galactic Odyssey" crew decided to press on, hoping that their camaraderie and shared determination would shield them from the obelisk's malevolent influence. As they prepared to unlock the secrets of the Forbidden Cosmos, the sense of suspense grew, and they braced themselves for the revelations and challenges that awaited them in the shadows of the enigmatic planet.

4

Cosmic Anomalies

The "Galactic Odyssey" crew gathered around the black obelisk, their faces determined despite the lingering unease caused by its malevolent influence. Captain Alex took a deep breath, trying to maintain focus amidst the strange energy emanating from the artifact.

"We must be cautious," he warned, "The ancient texts warned of immense power within the Forbidden Cosmos. We cannot let our curiosity cloud our judgment."

As they examined the obelisk, Science Officer Dr. Evelyn Alvarez noticed peculiar symbols etched into its surface. She began to decipher the cryptic markings, hoping to gain insight into its purpose.

"These symbols describe the Celestial Rift, a phenomenon beyond our current understanding of space-time," Dr. Alvarez explained. "It appears to be a tear in the fabric of reality, a gateway to unimaginable places."

The crew exchanged wary glances, realizing the gravity of the situation. The Celestial Rift could hold the key to unlocking the mysteries of the universe, but it could also lead to perilous consequences.

As they continued their investigation, the obelisk began to resonate with a low hum. A series of cosmic anomalies manifested around them, distorting space and time. Stars shimmered and vanished, only to reappear seconds later. Gravitational forces pulled in unexpected directions, and the crew struggled to maintain their footing.

"These anomalies are unlike anything I've ever seen," Lieutenant Ramirez exclaimed, trying to stabilize the ship's systems as they encountered the disturbances.

The "Galactic Odyssey" was caught in a swirling maelstrom of cosmic turbulence, and it was becoming increasingly clear that they had stumbled upon something far more profound than they could have imagined.

Amidst the chaos, the crew members experienced surreal visions—temporal loops, alternate realities, and glimpses of distant galaxies. The obelisk's influence intensified, attempting to lure them into the enigmatic Celestial Rift.

Captain Alex fought to keep his mind clear, rallying the crew to resist the temptations. "Focus on the mission! We cannot let this cosmic turbulence consume us," he urged, leading by example.

With their unity and determination, the crew managed to withstand the onslaught of the anomalies, and the obelisk's power began to wane. Dr. Alvarez identified a sequence of symbols that could potentially stabilize the rift.

Working together, they inputted the sequence into the obelisk, hoping it would reveal more answers than questions. The artifact responded with a brilliant surge of energy, and the rift expanded, revealing glimpses of unknown galaxies beyond.

Unveiled before them was a breathtaking cosmic tapestry, a canvas of unexplored worlds and celestial wonders. But it was also fraught with danger, as the fabric of reality quivered on the brink of collapse.

"We have opened a gateway to the unknown," Dr. Alvarez warned. "Whatever lies beyond is beyond our comprehension. We must proceed with caution."

With the rift stabilized, the crew peered into the abyss, contemplating the choice ahead of them. The allure of exploration beckoned, but the price of unraveling the Celestial Rift remained uncertain.

"We cannot let this power fall into the wrong hands," Commander Lee asserted. "We must seal the rift and safeguard the galaxy from its potential threats."

Captain Alex agreed, acknowledging the risks they faced. "Seal the rift," he commanded, "Our mission remains to protect and preserve the galaxy, and this knowledge is not something we're ready to wield."

As the crew worked together to seal the rift, the black obelisk finally fell silent, its malevolent influence dissipating. The sense of suspense began to lift, replaced with a newfound appreciation for the responsibility they bore.

Exiting the planet's surface, the "Galactic Odyssey" set a course for home, carrying with them the knowledge of the Celestial Rift and the mysteries they had encountered. The crew had faced cosmic anomalies and the pull of the unknown, but their unity and resilience had prevailed.

Yet, as they journeyed back to familiar territories, they couldn't shake the feeling that the universe still held countless secrets waiting to be discovered. And as the stars sparkled in the distance, the crew knew that their galactic odyssey was far from over, and that the next chapter would bring even more suspense and adventure.

5

The Betrayal

With the knowledge of the Celestial Rift safely sealed away, the "Galactic Odyssey" resumed its expedition, continuing to traverse the uncharted regions of the cosmos. The crew had overcome cosmic anomalies and the temptations of the enigmatic obelisk, strengthening their resolve and unity in the face of uncertainty.

As days turned into weeks, trust seemed to be restored among the crew, and they focused on their mission with renewed determination. However, unbeknownst to them, a subtle undercurrent of suspicion still lingered within their ranks.

Lieutenant Ramirez, the ship's communications expert, began to notice subtle irregularities in the ship's data logs. Small discrepancies in fuel consumption, navigational calculations, and even communication records raised an alarm in his mind.

"I can't be certain, but it looks like someone has been altering the ship's data," Ramirez reported to Captain Alex, his voice tinged with concern. "It's as if they're trying to cover their tracks."

Captain Alex's brow furrowed, the shadow of doubt once again casting its pall over the crew. "We must investigate this immediately. Check the security protocols and access logs. We need to know who might be tampering with our data."

Ramirez worked diligently, his fingers flying across the console to trace the source of the anomalies. As the hours passed, a disturbing discovery came to light—an encrypted transmission had been sent from the ship to an unknown destination.

"Captain," Ramirez's voice trembled, "Someone aboard the 'Galactic Odyssey' has been secretly communicating with an external party. I'm trying to trace the origin of the transmission, but the encryption is incredibly sophisticated."

Captain Alex's face tightened with concern. "This betrayal threatens not only our mission but the safety of the entire crew. We must act swiftly and decisively to uncover the traitor."

The captain convened an emergency meeting with Commander Lee, Dr. Alvarez, and Lieutenant Ramirez. Together, they formulated a plan to apprehend the perpetrator and put an end to the treachery that threatened their mission.

As the crew embarked on their internal investigation, tension filled the corridors of the starship. Whispers of suspicion circulated among the crew members, as each person wondered who could be capable of such deceit.

Commander Lee and Dr. Alvarez worked closely with the security team, analyzing the ship's surveillance footage and cross-referencing access logs. Their efforts led them to a surprising revelation—the encrypted transmission originated from Lieutenant Ramirez's workstation.

The discovery sent shockwaves through the crew. Ramirez was a well-respected and dedicated officer who had been with them since the beginning of the expedition. The accusations seemed inconceivable.

Captain Alex approached Ramirez with a heavy heart, "Lieutenant, we have evidence pointing to your involvement in this betrayal. Is there something you wish to tell us?"

Ramirez's eyes widened with disbelief, "Captain, I swear I have no idea how this could have happened. I would never betray this crew or jeopardize our mission."

Dr. Alvarez interjected, "Lieutenant, the evidence is compelling. We need to understand what's going on."

As the interrogation continued, Lieutenant Ramirez became increasingly agitated, struggling to explain the incriminating evidence against him. The crew watched in a mix of disbelief and sorrow as the truth gradually unraveled.

Ramirez revealed that he had been contacted by an anonymous party who claimed to hold information about his long-lost sister, whom he had been searching for throughout the expedition. Desperate to find his sibling, he had agreed to transmit classified data from the ship in exchange for the information.

"I never meant to harm the crew or the mission," Ramirez said, his voice shaking with regret. "I thought I was doing what was right for my family."

Captain Alex's heart went out to Ramirez, understanding the desperation that led him down this path. Nevertheless, the betrayal had endangered the entire crew and compromised the mission.

"Lieutenant, your actions have consequences," Captain Alex said with a heavy sigh. "You will face the appropriate repercussions, but we'll also try to find a way to help you locate your sister legally and safely."

As the "Galactic Odyssey" dealt with the aftermath of the betrayal, the crew grappled with a mix of emotions—sadness for Ramirez's predicament, yet a renewed commitment to uphold the trust and unity that had carried them so far. The journey continued, but the crew now knew that even amidst the vastness of the cosmos, the greatest challenges they faced might come from within.

6

The Celestial Abyss

The aftermath of Lieutenant Ramirez's betrayal left a somber atmosphere aboard the "Galactic Odyssey." The crew continued their expedition, but the sense of trust and camaraderie that once bound them together had been shaken. The journey through uncharted territory grew more tense as they approached an area of space known only as the Celestial Abyss.

The Celestial Abyss was a region where stars disappeared, swallowed by an inexplicable darkness. It was a void that seemed to defy the laws of physics, challenging the crew's understanding of the cosmos. The ship's sensors detected strange gravitational fluctuations and unpredictable cosmic storms, warning of the danger that lay ahead.

"Captain, I must caution against entering the Celestial Abyss," Science Officer Dr. Evelyn Alvarez urged, her voice laced with concern. "Our current knowledge is inadequate to predict what awaits us there."

Captain Alex nodded, acknowledging the gravity of the situation. "I share your concerns, Dr. Alvarez. However, we cannot turn away now. The mysteries of the cosmos beckon us onward, and we must face the unknown."

As the "Galactic Odyssey" approached the event horizon of the Celestial Abyss, tension gripped the crew. Whispers of fear and doubt echoed through the corridors, but they knew there was no turning back.

Commander Lee addressed the crew with a firm resolve, "We are explorers, adventurers. We've faced trials and tribulations before, and we'll face them again. Together, we shall navigate this abyss and emerge stronger for it."

As the starship crossed the threshold of the Celestial Abyss, the laws of physics seemed to unravel. Time warped, and the concept of distance became inconceivable. The crew braced themselves for the unpredictable nature of this cosmic enigma.

Cosmic storms raged outside the ship's protective shields, and stars vanished and reappeared in the blink of an eye. The crew struggled to maintain their bearings, relying on their training and collective experience to keep the "Galactic Odyssey" steady.

In the midst of the turmoil, they encountered celestial phenomena never before witnessed—nebulae of shifting colors, seemingly sentient pulsars, and bizarre celestial entities. Each moment was an assault on their senses, challenging their understanding of reality.

As days turned into what felt like an eternity, the crew's mental and physical endurance was pushed to its limits. Sleep became elusive as they battled the abyss's disorienting effects. Despite the challenges, their collective determination kept them moving forward.

Amidst the chaos, Captain Alex and the crew experienced vivid visions and haunting apparitions. Memories of their past resurfaced, and they confronted unresolved traumas and fears. The Celestial Abyss seemed to be probing their very souls, extracting emotions buried deep within.

"We must stay grounded in reality," Dr. Alvarez advised, "These visions are not real, merely manifestations of the abyss's influence."

Together, they supported each other through the psychological onslaught, determined not to be consumed by the darkness. Their unity and trust became their shield against the abyss's malevolence.

The crew's resilience was put to the ultimate test when the ship's systems started to falter under the stress. Critical components began to malfunction, and they faced the very real possibility of being stranded in this cosmic void.

"We can't let despair consume us," Lieutenant Ramirez said, his voice resolute despite the burden of his past actions. "We've overcome immense challenges before, and we'll overcome this one as well."

Working tirelessly, the crew managed to stabilize the ship's systems just in time, narrowly escaping the clutches of the Celestial Abyss. As they emerged on the other side, they felt a sense of accomplishment and a newfound understanding of the universe's mysteries.

The journey through the Celestial Abyss had left an indelible mark on the crew of the "Galactic Odyssey." They had faced darkness both within and without, testing the limits of their courage and camaraderie. Yet, they emerged stronger and more united, ready to face whatever lay ahead in their odyssey through the vastness of space. As they set course for the next uncharted frontier, the crew knew that their journey was far from over, and the cosmos held many more enigmas and wonders waiting to be discovered.

7

Unraveling the Enigma

The "Galactic Odyssey" emerged from the Celestial Abyss, forever changed by their harrowing journey through the cosmic void. The crew had faced their deepest fears and confronted the mysteries of the universe, but their quest for the Celestial Key was far from over.

With renewed determination, they continued their expedition, now equipped with invaluable knowledge and a stronger bond forged in the crucible of adversity. Captain Alex knew that they were on the brink of something extraordinary, and they had to be prepared for whatever awaited them.

As they charted a course deeper into unexplored territory, Science Officer Dr. Evelyn Alvarez made a startling discovery. She found ancient records in the ship's archives that spoke of a fabled artifact—the "Astra Codex." The codex was said to hold the knowledge of the Celestial Key's true nature and how to unlock its potential.

"This could be the breakthrough we've been searching for," Dr. Alvarez shared with the crew. "The Astra Codex may hold the key to understanding the enigma that has guided our journey."

The crew rallied behind the newfound hope, setting their sights on locating the Astra Codex. Their journey led them to a distant, enigmatic planet known as "Nirvana Prime," a world steeped in legends of ancient civilizations and lost knowledge.

Upon landing, the crew encountered a breathtaking landscape—luminous flora, sentient crystal formations, and a serene atmosphere that seemed to imbue a sense of tranquility. However, beneath the planet's tranquil exterior lay echoes of a forgotten power.

Guided by the clues found within the codex, the crew ventured into the heart of Nirvana Prime's ruins, searching for the ancient repository of knowledge. Each step they took seemed to unravel the planet's enigmatic history, hinting at an ancient cosmic civilization that had transcended the boundaries of time and space.

As they delved deeper, they found themselves facing tests of intellect and courage—cryptic puzzles, surreal riddles, and cosmic gateways that challenged their understanding of reality. The planet seemed to test their worthiness to access the Astra Codex.

Commander Lee's diplomacy skills were put to the test as he navigated a complex negotiation with an ethereal guardian of the codex. Dr. Alvarez deciphered ancient scripts with her brilliant mind, unlocking the secrets of the planet's cosmic knowledge.

Finally, at the heart of Nirvana Prime's ruins, they stood before the Astra Codex—an ethereal, luminescent orb that seemed to radiate with the wisdom of the cosmos.

As the crew gazed upon the Astra Codex, they felt an inexplicable connection to the universe, a sense of unity with the stars themselves. The codex's knowledge flooded their minds, revealing the truth behind the Celestial Key.

The Celestial Key was not a physical object or artifact. It was a metaphorical representation of cosmic knowledge—the collective wisdom of all civilizations that had ever explored the universe. The true power of the Celestial Key lay in the understanding of the interconnectedness of all life and the responsibility to protect and preserve the delicate balance of the cosmos.

With this revelation, the crew understood that their journey was not about obtaining a physical prize but embracing the journey itself—the pursuit of knowledge, unity, and the courage to face the unknown.

As they returned to the "Galactic Odyssey," Captain Alex addressed the crew, "We may not have found a tangible key, but we have discovered something far more profound—the wisdom to respect the mysteries of the universe and the responsibility to safeguard its harmony."

The crew nodded in agreement, their hearts filled with a sense of fulfillment that transcended any physical reward. They had grown not only as individuals but as a united force capable of confronting the vastness of the cosmos.

As the starship set its course for home, the crew knew that their odyssey was far from over. The journey to explore the infinite reaches of space would continue, but now armed with the wisdom of the Astra Codex, they embraced the suspense and the wonders that lay ahead with open hearts and steadfast resolve.

8

Galactic Showdown

With the wisdom of the Astra Codex imprinted on their minds and a newfound sense of purpose, the "Galactic Odyssey" embarked on the next phase of their expedition. Their journey through the uncharted regions of space had led them to the realization that their quest for knowledge and unity was intertwined with the fate of the entire galaxy.

As they ventured deeper into unexplored territories, they encountered various factions vying for supremacy and control over valuable resources. Their rivals, the "Cosmic Consortium," were known for their cutthroat tactics and willingness to exploit any advantage they could find.

"We must be vigilant," Commander Lee warned the crew during a strategy meeting. "The knowledge we possess makes us both valuable and vulnerable. The Cosmic Consortium will not hesitate to seize any opportunity to gain the upper hand."

The crew agreed, understanding the stakes of their mission. The knowledge they carried was a beacon that could either guide civilizations towards enlightenment or unleash chaos if it fell into the wrong hands.

Their suspicions were confirmed when they intercepted a coded transmission indicating that the Cosmic Consortium had learned of their discoveries, including the Astra Codex. The rivals were closing in, seeking to seize the wisdom the "Galactic Odyssey" held.

"We cannot allow them to take the knowledge from us," Dr. Alvarez asserted. "Our duty is to protect and share this wisdom for the betterment of the galaxy."

Captain Alex nodded in agreement, "We must stay one step ahead. Prepare the ship's defenses, and let's be ready for any confrontation."

As the "Galactic Odyssey" continued its expedition, the tension aboard the ship heightened. The crew's senses were on high alert as they navigated through cosmic obstacles and treacherous territories, wary of any signs of interference from the Cosmic Consortium.

One fateful day, their fears were realized when they found themselves surrounded by a fleet of Consortium warships. The rivals had intercepted their course, intending to capture the crew and claim the wisdom of the Astra Codex for themselves.

A tense standoff ensued as the rival ships encircled the "Galactic Odyssey," their weapons primed and ready for conflict. But Captain Alex knew that this confrontation could not be resolved with brute force alone.

"Open a channel to their flagship," Captain Alex ordered, "We need to talk."

Commander Lee initiated communication with the Consortium's leader, a ruthless and ambitious warlord named Zara Vex. The conversation was tense, with both sides unwilling to back down. However, Captain Alex appealed to the warlord's sense of reason, urging her to consider the implications of harnessing the knowledge they possessed.

"Our quest is not one of conquest," Captain Alex implored, "We seek to understand the cosmos, to foster unity among civilizations, and to protect the harmony of the galaxy. With the Astra Codex, we can work together towards a brighter future for all."

Zara Vex hesitated, torn between her ambitions and the weight of the captain's words. She had always sought power and control, but the notion of a greater purpose stirred something within her.

After a long pause, Zara finally spoke, "This is not over, Captain. But I will consider your proposition."

The Consortium warships slowly withdrew, leaving the "Galactic Odyssey" unharmed but still uncertain of their rival's intentions. Captain Alex knew that their peaceful approach might not have convinced Zara completely, but it was a step towards avoiding an all-out conflict.

As the crew continued their expedition, they remained vigilant. The threat of the Cosmic Consortium still loomed, but they had learned that their journey was not just about acquiring knowledge but about sharing it and fostering unity among civilizations.

Their mission had evolved from a search for a physical key to a quest for the understanding of the cosmos itself. The "Galactic Odyssey" had become a symbol of hope, and the crew was determined to safeguard the wisdom they carried, ensuring that it would guide the galaxy towards enlightenment rather than destruction.

With each passing day, the crew faced new challenges and encountered civilizations both advanced and primitive, each with its own unique perspective on the universe. As they continued their odyssey, they knew that their quest for knowledge and unity would be ongoing, and the suspense of the unknown would forever drive them to explore the infinite reaches of space.

9

The Galactic Assembly

As the "Galactic Odyssey" journeyed through the uncharted territories of space, the crew's reputation grew, and the wisdom they carried from the Astra Codex spread like a beacon of hope throughout the galaxy. Their quest for knowledge and unity had transcended the confines of their starship, inspiring civilizations far and wide.

Word of the "Galactic Odyssey" reached the ears of the wise and enigmatic leaders of the galaxy—the Galactic Assembly. This esteemed council consisted of representatives from various advanced civilizations, each dedicated to promoting harmony, knowledge-sharing, and cooperation among the stars.

The Assembly summoned the "Galactic Odyssey" to a momentous gathering—a rare occurrence that had only taken place on significant occasions in the history of the galaxy.

Upon their arrival, Captain Alex and the crew were greeted by a diverse array of beings, each emanating an aura of wisdom and experience. The council chambers were an awe-inspiring sight—a celestial amphitheater floating among the stars, an embodiment of the unity the Assembly sought to achieve.

"We have heard of your odyssey, your quest for knowledge and unity," spoke the head of the Assembly, a wise and ancient being known as the Elder Starshaper. "Your journey has rippled across the galaxy, and we wish to learn from the wisdom you have accumulated."

Captain Alex humbly addressed the assembly, "We are but explorers, seeking to understand the mysteries of the cosmos and to foster unity among civilizations. The knowledge we carry is not ours to hoard but to share with all who seek it."

The crew of the "Galactic Odyssey" stood before the Galactic Assembly, recounting their adventures, the challenges they had faced, and the wisdom they had gained from the Astra Codex. They shared their vision of a galaxy where knowledge was freely shared, and civilizations collaborated to better the lives of all sentient beings.

The assembly listened intently, and a sense of reverence permeated the atmosphere. The crew's message resonated deeply with the council members, and they saw the potential of the wisdom the "Galactic Odyssey" possessed to bring harmony and prosperity to the galaxy.

After careful deliberation, the Elder Starshaper spoke, "Your journey has shown us the power of knowledge, unity, and the pursuit of a higher purpose. The Galactic Assembly stands with you in fostering cooperation among civilizations and sharing the wisdom of the cosmos."

With these words, the "Galactic Odyssey" and its crew became honorary members of the Galactic Assembly—a rare honor bestowed upon those whose actions held the potential to shape the course of the galaxy.

The crew's journey had transcended beyond exploration—it had become a catalyst for change. They had united disparate civilizations, encouraging the exchange of knowledge and the embrace of diversity.

As they continued their expedition, they were no longer mere explorers but ambassadors of unity, spreading the message of the Galactic Assembly far and wide. They encountered new challenges and civilizations with an open mind, knowing that each encounter was an opportunity to learn and grow.

The "Galactic Odyssey" became a symbol of hope and inspiration, a testament to the power of cooperation and the pursuit of knowledge. As their quest continued, the crew knew that they were part of something greater—a cosmic symphony in which every being played a vital role.

In the end, their journey was not just about exploring the vastness of space; it was about exploring the boundless potential within each individual and civilization to contribute to the greater good.

The suspense-filled chapters of the "Galactic Odyssey" were etched into the annals of cosmic history—a tale of courage, camaraderie, and the unyielding spirit of exploration. The crew's legacy would endure for generations, inspiring countless beings to embark on their own odysseys, united in the pursuit of knowledge, harmony, and the mysteries of the cosmos.

10

Homecoming

After a remarkable journey filled with suspense, discovery, and unity, the "Galactic Odyssey" set a course for home—their journey through the uncharted regions of space had finally come to an end. As they approached the familiar territories of known space, a mix of emotions filled the hearts of the crew.

Captain Alex stood at the helm, gazing out at the stars that had been their constant companions throughout their odyssey. Memories of their adventures flooded his mind—the celestial wonders they had witnessed, the challenges they had overcome, and the unity they had forged.

"It's hard to believe that our journey is over," Lieutenant Ramirez said, joining the captain at the helm. "I will forever cherish the experiences we shared, the knowledge we gained, and the friendships we formed."

Captain Alex nodded, "Our journey has been transformative. We've learned that the pursuit of knowledge and unity can reshape the destiny of the entire galaxy. But our odyssey doesn't truly end here; it will continue within us and in the lives of those we've touched."

As the "Galactic Odyssey" approached the familiar sight of their home planet, a sense of anticipation and apprehension filled the crew. They wondered how their return would be received and what tales they would have to share with their loved ones and fellow citizens.

As they entered the planet's atmosphere, cheers erupted among the crew. The news of their return had spread, and the sight of the "Galactic Odyssey" descending from the heavens was met with awe and admiration from the people below.

Upon landing, the crew was greeted by a jubilant crowd, eager to hear their stories of adventure and discovery. They were celebrated as heroes, not only for their courage in exploring the unknown but also for their dedication to fostering unity among civilizations.

During a grand ceremony, Captain Alex addressed the gathered crowd, "We set out on this odyssey with a thirst for knowledge and a vision of unity among the stars. Our journey has shown us that the pursuit of wisdom and cooperation can overcome the boundaries that divide us."

The crew members were honored with medals of valor and recognition from various civilizations whose lives they had touched during their expedition. The sense of unity they had fostered had not only strengthened their own home planet but had rippled across the galaxy, igniting a desire for greater understanding and collaboration.

In the following weeks, the crew members reunited with their families and friends, sharing their tales of suspense, adventure, and the transformative power of their journey. The "Galactic Odyssey" had become more than just a starship; it had become a symbol of hope and inspiration.

With their mission accomplished, the crew of the "Galactic Odyssey" settled back into civilian life, but they remained connected by the bond they had forged during their expedition. They knew that their journey had changed them forever, and the wisdom they had gained would continue to guide their actions.

The legacy of the "Galactic Odyssey" lived on, inspiring future generations of explorers, scientists, and diplomats to continue seeking knowledge, fostering unity, and embracing the mysteries of the cosmos.

As the crew members went their separate ways, they knew that the journey was not over—it was merely a new beginning. Their hearts were filled with gratitude for the friendships they had formed, the wisdom they had gained, and the adventures that still awaited them among the stars.

And so, the "Galactic Odyssey" had left an indelible mark on the galaxy—the story of a courageous crew who had ventured into the unknown, faced their fears, and emerged with a deeper understanding of themselves and the universe.

Their journey may have concluded, but the spirit of exploration, unity, and wonder lived on, reminding all sentient beings that the pursuit of knowledge and harmony was a journey without end—a journey that would forever carry them toward the infinite horizons of the cosmos.

11

The Eternal Odyssey

Years had passed since the crew of the "Galactic Odyssey" returned home as celebrated heroes. Their epic journey had left an enduring legacy in the annals of cosmic history. The spirit of exploration, unity, and knowledge-sharing they had fostered had sparked a new era of interstellar cooperation.

The wisdom they had gained from the Astra Codex continued to guide civilizations toward a brighter future, as the Galactic Assembly worked together to tackle challenges, share advancements, and preserve the harmony of the galaxy.

The crew members had taken different paths, pursuing their passions and contributing to the galaxy in diverse ways. Commander Lee had become an ambassador, fostering diplomacy and understanding among civilizations. Lieutenant Ramirez had become a mentor to young explorers, sharing his experiences and teaching them the value of unity.

Dr. Evelyn Alvarez had become a renowned scientist, leading groundbreaking research that pushed the boundaries of cosmic knowledge. Captain Alex, ever the visionary, had dedicated himself to promoting galactic education and inspiring future generations to reach for the stars.

Their stories had become legends, inspiring countless beings to embark on their own journeys of exploration and enlightenment. The "Galactic Odyssey" had transformed from a starship into a symbol of hope—an enduring testament to the power of unity and the pursuit of knowledge.

As the years turned into centuries, the crew's memory lived on, and the stories of their odyssey passed through generations. The spirit of adventure and the quest for wisdom remained a driving force, shaping the destiny of civilizations and drawing them together in a cosmic tapestry of cooperation.

And so, the "Galactic Odyssey" embarked on an eternal journey, forever etched in the cosmos—a timeless reminder that the pursuit of knowledge, unity, and understanding was a quest without end. As new explorers took to the stars, their hearts were filled with the legacy of the brave crew who had journeyed into the unknown, forever guiding them toward the infinite horizons of the universe.

The odyssey had no end, for the mysteries of the cosmos were boundless, and the pursuit of knowledge was an eternal adventure. And as the stars sparkled in the distant night sky, the spirit of the "Galactic Odyssey" lived on, inspiring all sentient beings to embrace the suspense, wonder, and harmony of the cosmic symphony that unfolded before them.

Printed by BoD™ in Norderstedt, Germany

9 788147 835648